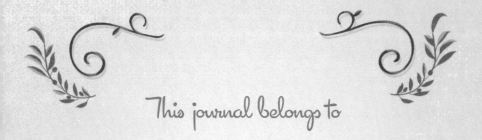

This journal belongs to

....

Date

....

The God who created, names, and numbers the stars in the heavens also numbers the hairs of my head.... He pays attention to very big things and to very small ones. What matters to me matters to Him, and that changes my life.

ELISABETH ELLIOT

Better is one day with God than a thousand days without Him.

Life is rarely easy, but when you let God in, your perspective changes. He begins to work out things in your life like contentment, love, joy, grace, and rest. He does this for you, His child, simply because He loves you. Through all your days—the good ones, the bad ones, the joy-filled, the tear-filled—God is right by your side, giving, providing, helping you in each and every moment.

He cares for you. He loves you. He listens to you. Pour out your heart to Him about all you are facing today, and be encouraged as you read quotations and verses that will remind you of His presence. Life isn't perfect, but with God, it is better.

I delight in your unfailing love, God. No matter where I go, it surrounds me.

Your love, LORD, reaches to the heavens, your faithfulness to the skies.
Your righteousness is like the highest mountains, your justice like
the great deep.... How priceless is your unfailing love, O God!

PSALM 36:5–7 NIV

When we allow God the privilege of shaping our lives, we discover new depths of purpose and meaning. What a joyful thought to realize you are a chosen vessel for God— perfectly suited for His use.

JONI EARECKSON TADA

It is clear to us, friends, that God not only loves you very much but also has put his hand on you for something special.

1 THESSALONIANS 1:4 MSG

God will never, never, never let us down if we have faith...in Him. He will always look after us. So we must cleave to Jesus. Our whole life must simply be woven into Jesus.

MOTHER TERESA

Know therefore that the LORD your God is God; he is the faithful God,
keeping his covenant of love to a thousand generations of those who
love him and keep his commandments.

DEUTERONOMY 7:9 NIV

Peace *with* God brings the peace *of* God. It is a peace that settles our nerves, fills our mind, floods our spirit, and in the midst of the uproar around us, gives us the assurance that everything is all right.

BOB MUMFORD

May the God of hope fill you with all joy and peace as you trust in him, so that you may overflow with hope.

ROMANS 15:13 NIV

It is an extraordinary and beautiful thing that God, in creation...works with the beauty of matter; the reality of things; the discoveries of the senses, all five of them; so that we, in turn, may hear the grass growing; see a face springing to life in love and laughter.... The offerings of creation...our glimpses of truth.

MADELEINE L'ENGLE

Honor and majesty surround him; strength and beauty fill his sanctuary.

Live today! Live fully each moment of today. Trust God to let you work through this moment and the next. He will give you all you need. Don't skip over the painful or confusing moment—even it has its important and rightful place in the day.

May Jesus himself and God our Father, who reached out in love and surprised you with gifts of unending help and confidence, put a fresh heart in you, invigorate your work, enliven your speech.

2 THESSALONIANS 2:16–17 MSG

*O the pure delight of a single hour
That before Thy throne I spend,
When I kneel in prayer, and with Thee, my God,
I commune as friend with friend!*

FANNY J. CROSBY

Let the godly rejoice. Let them be glad in God's presence.
Let them be filled with joy.

He is the Source. Of everything. Strength for your day. Wisdom for your task. Comfort for your soul. Grace for your battle. Provision for each need. Understanding for each failure. Assistance for every encounter.

JACK HAYFORD

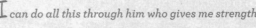

I can do all this through him who gives me strength.

PHILIPPIANS 4:13 NIV

Lift up your eyes. Your heavenly Father waits to bless you—in inconceivable ways to make your life what you never dreamed it could be.

ANNE ORTLUND

God's blessing makes life rich; nothing we do can improve on God.

PROVERBS 10:22 MSG

God's holy beauty comes near you, like a spiritual scent, and it stirs your drowsing soul.... He creates in you the desire to find Him and run after Him—to follow wherever He leads you, and to press peacefully against His heart wherever He is.

JOHN OF THE CROSS

How lovely is your dwelling place, LORD Almighty! My soul yearns, even faints, for the courts of the LORD.... Blessed are those who dwell in your house; they are ever praising you.... Better is one day in your courts than a thousand elsewhere.

PSALM 84:1-2, 4, 10 NIV

Happiness is found in relationships. And life's greatest happiness is found in life's greatest relationship: a personal relationship with God through Jesus Christ.

KENNETH L. TANGEN

May you experience the love of Christ, though it is too great to understand fully. Then you will be made complete with all the fullness of life and power that comes from God.

EPHESIANS 3:19 NLT

The Creator of all thinks enough of you to have sent Someone very special so that you might have life—abundantly, joyfully, completely, and victoriously.

KARL BARTH

*God's gift has restored our relationship with him and given us back our lives.
And there's more life to come—an eternity of life! You can count on this.*

TITUS 3:7 MSG

If you have a special need today, focus your full attention on the goodness and greatness of your Father rather than on the size of your need. Your need is so small compared to His ability to meet it.

Let us come boldly to the throne of our gracious God. There we will receive his mercy, and we will find grace to help us when we need it most.

HEBREWS 4:16 NLT

The beauty of the earth, the beauty of the sky, the order of the stars, the sun, the moon...their very loveliness is their confession of God: for who made these lovely mutable things, but He who is Himself unchangeable beauty?

Augustine

Wilderness and desert will sing joyously, the badlands will celebrate and flower—
Like the crocus in spring, bursting into blossom, a symphony of song and color.
Mountain glories of Lebanon—a gift. Awesome Carmel, stunning Sharon—gifts.
GOD's resplendent glory, fully on display. GOD awesome, GOD majestic.

ISAIAH 35:1-2 MSG

My Lord God, I have no idea where I am going. I do not see the road ahead of me.... But I believe that the desire to please You does in fact please You.... You will lead me by the right road.... I trust You always though I may seem to be lost.... You will never leave me to face my perils alone.

THOMAS MERTON

I am always with you; you hold me by my right hand.

PSALM 73:23 NIV

The God of peace gives perfect peace to those whose hearts are stayed upon Him.

CHARLES H. SPURGEON

I am leaving you with a gift—peace of mind and heart. And the peace I give is a gift the world cannot give. So don't be troubled or afraid.

Faith in God gives your life a center from which you can reach out and dare to love the world.

BARBARA FARMER

Whoever believes in me, as Scripture has said, rivers of living water will flow from within them.

JOHN 7:38 NIV

Let God have you, and let God love you—and don't be surprised if your heart begins to hear music you've never heard and your feet learn to dance as never before.

MAX LUCADO

Sing songs to the tune of his glory, set glory to the rhythms of his praise.

The love of the Father is like a sudden rain shower that will pour forth when you least expect it, catching you up into wonder and praise.

RICHARD J. FOSTER

See what great love the Father has lavished on us, that we should be called children of God! And that is what we are!

1 JOHN 3:1 NIV

Do not be afraid to enter the cloud that is settling down on your life. God is in it. The other side is radiant with His glory.

L. B. COWMAN

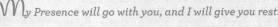

My Presence will go with you, and I will give you rest.

EXODUS 33:14 NIV

You are in the Beloved...therefore infinitely dear to the Father, unspeakably precious to Him. You are never, not for one second, alone.

NORMAN DOWTY

For you are my hiding place; you protect me from trouble. You surround me with songs of victory. The LORD says, "I will guide you along the best pathway for your life. I will advise you and watch over you."

PSALM 32:7–8 NLT

God still draws near to us in the ordinary, commonplace, everyday experiences and places.... He comes in surprising ways.

HENRY GARIEPY

Show me the wonders of your great love.... Keep me as the apple of your eye; hide me in the shadow of your wings.

Allow your dreams a place in your prayers and plans. God-given dreams can help you move into the future He is preparing for you.

"For I know the plans I have for you," declares the Lord, "plans to prosper you and not to harm you, plans to give you hope and a future."

JEREMIAH 29:11 NIV

All perfect gifts are from above and all our blessings show the amplitude of God's dear love, which any heart may know.

LAURA LEE RANDALL

Bless the LORD, O my soul; and all that is within me, bless His holy name! Bless the LORD, O my soul, and forget not all His benefits.... who crowns you with lovingkindness and tender mercies, who satisfies your mouth with good things, so that your youth is renewed like the eagle's.

PSALM 103:1–3, 4–5 NKJV

God's nature is given me. His love is jealous for my life. All His attributes are woven into the pattern of my spirit. What a God is this! His life implanted in every child. Thank You, Father, for this.

JIM ELLIOT

The Lord is like a father to his children, tender and compassionate to those who fear him.... The love of the Lord remains forever.

PSALM 103:13, 17 NLT

Genuine heart-hunger, accompanied by sincere seeking after eternal values, does not go unrewarded.

JUSTINE KNIGHT

Blessed are those who hunger and thirst for righteousness, for they will be filled.

We must drink deeply from the very Source the deep calm and peace of interior quietude and refreshment of God, allowing the pure water of divine grace to flow plentifully and unceasingly from the Source itself.

MOTHER TERESA

The Lᴏʀᴅ will guide you always; he will satisfy your needs in a
sun-scorched land and will strengthen your frame. You will be like
a well-watered garden, like a spring whose waters never fail.

Iꜱᴀɪᴀʜ 58:11 ɴɪᴠ

Today I give it all to Jesus...my hopes, my plans and dreams and schemes, my fears and failures—all. Peace and contentment come when the struggle ceases.

GLORIA GAITHER

I have told you these things, so that in me you may have peace. In this world you will have trouble. But take heart! I have overcome the world.

A living, loving God can and does make His presence felt, can and does speak to us in the silence of our hearts, can and does warm and caress us till we no longer doubt that He is near, that He is here.

BRENNAN MANNING

Many, O Lord my God, are the wonders which You have done, and Your thoughts toward us; there is none to compare with You. If I would declare and speak of them, they would be too numerous to count.

PSALM 40:5 NASB

When God has become...our refuge and our fortress, then we can reach out to Him in the midst of a broken world and feel at home while still on the way.

HENRI J. M. NOUWEN

Hear my cry, O God; give heed to my prayer. From the end of the earth
I call to You when my heart is faint; lead me to the rock that is higher than I.
For You have been a refuge for me, a tower of strength against the enemy.
Let me...take refuge in the shelter of Your wings.

PSALM 61:1–4 NASB

Life need not be easy to be joyful. Joy is not the absence of trouble, but the presence of Christ.

WILLIAM VANDERHOVEN

I know the LORD is always with me. I will not be shaken,
for he is right beside me. No wonder my heart is glad, and I rejoice.

PSALM 16:8–9 NLT

Nothing can separate you from His love, absolutely nothing.... God is enough for time, and God is enough for eternity. God is enough!

HANNAH WHITALL SMITH

Neither death nor life, neither angels nor demons, neither the present nor the future, nor any powers, neither height nor depth, nor anything else in all creation, will be able to separate us from the love of God that is in Christ Jesus our Lord.

ROMANS 8:35, 37–39 NIV

So wait before the Lord. Wait in the stillness. And in that stillness, assurance will come to you. You will know that you are heard; you will know that your Lord ponders the voice of your humble desires; you will hear quiet words spoken to you yourself, perhaps to your grateful surprise and refreshment.

AMY CARMICHAEL

I prayed to the LORD, and He answered me. He freed me from all my fears. Those who look to him for help will be radiant with joy.

God loves to look at us, and loves it when we will look back at Him. Even when we try to run away from our troubles...God will find us, bless us, even when we feel most alone, unsure.... God will find a way to let us know that He is with us in this place, wherever we are.

KATHLEEN NORRIS

If I rise on the wings of the dawn, if I settle on the far side of the sea, even there your hand will guide me, your right hand will hold me fast.

PSALM 139:9–10 NIV

A quiet morning with a loving God puts the events of the upcoming day into proper perspective.

JANETTE OKE

In the morning, LORD, you hear my voice; in the morning I lay my requests before you and wait expectantly.

PSALM 5:3 NIV

God cares for the world He created, from the rising of a nation to the falling of the sparrow. Everything in the world lies under the watchful gaze of His providential eyes, from the numbering of the days of our life to the numbering of the hairs on our head.

KEN GIRE

Look at the birds of the air, that they do not sow, nor reap nor gather into barns, and yet your heavenly Father feeds them. Are you not worth much more than they?

MATTHEW 6:26 NASB

All that is good, all that is true, all that is beautiful, all that is beneficent, be it great or small, be it perfect or fragmentary, natural as well as supernatural, moral as well as material, comes from God.

JOHN HENRY NEWMAN

Oh, put God to the test and see how kind he is! See for yourself the way his mercies shower down on all who trust in him. If you belong to the Lord, reverence him; for everyone who does this has everything he needs.

PSALM 34:8–9 TLB

Faith allows us to continually delight in life since we have placed our needs in God's hands.

JANET L. SMITH

Faith is the confidence that what we hope for will actually happen; it gives us assurance about things we cannot see.

HEBREWS 11:1 NLT

When God finds a soul that rests in Him and is not easily moved...
to this same soul He gives the joy of His presence.

CATHERINE OF GENOA

You're my place of quiet retreat; I wait for your Word to renew me....
I lovingly embrace everything you say.

PSALM 119:114, 119 MSG

Just as there comes a warm sunbeam into every cottage window, so comes a love-beam of God's care for every separate need.

NATHANIEL HAWTHORNE

I am the light of the world. Whoever follows me will never walk in darkness, but will have the light of life.

JOHN 8:12 NIV

Like supernatural effervescence, praise will sometimes bubble up from the joy of simply knowing Christ. Praise like that is...delight. Pure pleasure!

JONI EARECKSON TADA

Our mouths were filled with laughter, our tongues with songs of joy....
The Lord has done great things for us, and we are filled with joy.

PSALM 126:2–3 NIV

*God's love is like a river springing up in the Divine
Substance and flowing endlessly through His creation,
filling all things with life and goodness and strength.*

THOMAS MERTON

Creation and creatures applaud you, GOD; your holy people bless you.
They talk about the glories of your rule, they exclaim over your splendor....
Generous to a fault, you lavish your favor on all creatures.
Everything GOD does is right—the trademark on all his works is love.

PSALM 145:10–11, 16–17 MSG

Whatever the circumstances, whatever the call...His strength will be your strength in your hour of need.

BILLY GRAHAM

Ah, Sovereign Lord, you have made the heavens and the earth by your great power and outstretched arm. Nothing is too hard for you.

God may be invisible, but He's in touch. You may not be able to see Him, but He is in control. And that includes you—your circumstances. That includes what you've just lost. That includes what you've just gained. That includes all of life—past, present, future.

CHARLES R. SWINDOLL

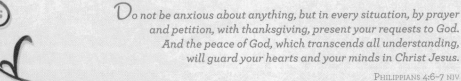

Do not be anxious about anything, but in every situation, by prayer and petition, with thanksgiving, present your requests to God. And the peace of God, which transcends all understanding, will guard your hearts and your minds in Christ Jesus.

PHILIPPIANS 4:6–7 NIV

Only God gives true peace—a quiet gift He sets within us just when we think we've exhausted our search for it.

*You will keep in perfect peace all who trust in you,
all whose thoughts are fixed on you!*

ISAIAH 26:3 NLT

Beauty puts a face on God. When we gaze at nature, at a loved one, at a work of art, our soul immediately recognizes and is drawn to the face of God.

MARGARET BROWNLEY

Let the beauty of the LORD our God be upon us,
and establish the work of our hands for us.

PSALM 90:17 NKJV

The Lord's chief desire is to reveal Himself to you and, in order for Him to do that, He gives you abundant grace. The Lord gives you the experience of enjoying His presence. He touches you, and His touch is so delightful that, more than ever, you are drawn inwardly to Him.

MADAME JEANNE GUYON

O God, you are my God; I earnestly search for you. My soul thirsts for you; my whole body longs for you in this parched and weary land where there is no water. I have seen you in your sanctuary and gazed upon your power and glory. Your unfailing love is better than life itself.

PSALM 63:1-3 NLT

We have a Father in heaven who is almighty, who loves
His children as He loves His only-begotten Son, and whose
very joy and delight it is to...help them at all times and
under all circumstances.

GEORGE MUELLER

I will lift up my eyes to the hills—
From whence comes my help?
My help comes from the LORD,
Who made heaven and earth.

PSALM 121:1–2 NKJV

Be still, and in the quiet moments, listen to the voice of your heavenly Father. His words can renew your spirit.... No one knows you and your needs like He does.

JANET L. SMITH

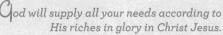

God will supply all your needs according to His riches in glory in Christ Jesus.

PHILIPPIANS 4:19 NASB

All [God's] glory and beauty come from within, and there He delights to dwell. His visits there are frequent, His conversation sweet, His comforts refreshing, His peace passing all understanding.

THOMAS À KEMPIS

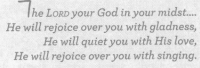

The LORD your God in your midst....
He will rejoice over you with gladness,
He will quiet you with His love,
He will rejoice over you with singing.

ZEPHANIAH 3:17 NJKV

Always new. Always exciting. Always full of promise. The mornings of our lives, each a personal daily miracle!

GLORIA GAITHER

The LORD's lovingkindnesses indeed never cease,
For His compassions never fail.
They are new every morning;
Great is Your faithfulness.

LAMENTATIONS 3:22–23 NASB

Let's praise His name! He is holy, He is almighty.
He is love. He brings hope, forgiveness, heart cleansing,
peace and power. He is our deliverer and coming King.
Praise His wonderful name!

LUCILLE M. LAW

May you be filled with joy, always thanking the Father. He has enabled you to share in the inheritance that belongs to his people, who live in the light.

COLOSSIANS 1:11–12 NLT

To pray is to change. *This is a great grace.* How good of God to provide a path whereby our lives can be taken over by love and joy and peace and patience and kindness and goodness and faithfulness and gentleness and self-control.

RICHARD J. FOSTER

I *will give you a new heart and put a new spirit in you.*

A new path lies before us; we're not sure where it leads;
But God goes on before us, providing all our needs.
This path, so new, so different, exciting as we climb,
Will guide us in His perfect will until the end of time.

LINDA MAURICE

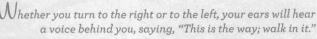

Whether you turn to the right or to the left, your ears will hear a voice behind you, saying, "This is the way; walk in it."

ISAIAH 30:21 NIV

When we focus on God, the scene changes. He's in control of our lives; nothing lies outside the realm of His redemptive grace. Even when we make mistakes, fail in relationships, or deliberately make bad choices, God can redeem us.

PENELOPE J. STOKES

He is merciful and tender toward those who don't deserve it;
he is slow to get angry and full of kindness and love.

PSALM 103:8 TLB

The God of the universe—the One who created everything and holds it all in His hands—created each of us in His image, to bear His likeness, His imprint. It is only when Christ dwells within our hearts, radiating the pure light of His love through our humanity that we discover who we are and what we were intended to be.

WENDY MOORE

Ask the God of our Master, Jesus Christ...to make you intelligent and discerning in knowing him personally, your eyes focused and clear, so that you can see exactly what it is he is calling you to do, grasp the immensity of this glorious way of life he has for his followers.

EPHESIANS 1:17–18 MSG

Few delights can equal the mere presence of one whom we trust utterly.

GEORGE MacDONALD

Take delight in the LORD, and he will give you your heart's desires.
Commit everything you do to the LORD. Trust him, and he will help you.

PSALM 37:4–5 NLT

I would rather walk with God in the dark than go alone in the light.

MARY GARDINER BRAINARD

Don't be afraid, I've redeemed you. I've called your name. You're mine. When you're in over your head, I'll be there with you.... When you're between a rock and a hard place, it won't be a dead end—because I am GOD, your personal God.... I paid a huge price for you...! That's how much you mean to me! That's how much I love you!

ISAIAH 43:1–4 MSG

We encounter God in the ordinariness of life, not in the search for spiritual highs and extraordinary, mystical experiences, but in our simple presence in life.

BRENNAN MANNING

You make known to me the path of life; you will fill me with joy in your presence, with eternal pleasures at your right hand.

PSALM 16:11 NIV

[God] delights to meet the faith of one who looks up to Him and says, "Lord, You know that I cannot do this—but I believe that You can!"

Amy Carmichael

The Lord is the everlasting God, the Creator of all the earth. He never grows weak or weary.... Even youths will become weak and tired.... But those who trust in the Lord will find new strength. They will soar high on wings like eagles. They will run and not grow weary. They will walk and not faint.

ISAIAH 40:28, 30-31 NLT

The joyful birds prolong the strain,
their song with every spring renewed;
the air we breathe, and falling rain,
each softly whispers: God is good.

SIR JOHN HAMDEN GURNEY

Mostly what God does is love you. Keep company with him and
learn a life of love. Observe how Christ loved us. His love was not
cautious but extravagant. He didn't love in order to get something
from us but to give everything of himself to us. Love like that.

EPHESIANS 5:1-2 MSG

Humor is one of God's most marvelous gifts. Humor gives us smiles, laughter, and gaiety. Humor reveals the roses and hides the thorns. Humor makes our heavy burdens light and smoothes the rough spots in our pathways.

SAM ERVIN

A cheerful heart is good medicine.

When we call on God, He bends down His ear to listen,
as a father bends down to listen to his little child.

ELIZABETH CHARLES

I call on you, my God, for you will answer me;
turn your ear to me and hear my prayer.

PSALM 17:6 NIV

Into all our lives, in many simple, familiar, homely ways, God infuses this element of joy from the surprises of life, which unexpectedly brighten our days, and fill our eyes with light.

Samuel Longfellow

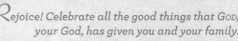

Rejoice! Celebrate all the good things that GOD, your God, has given you and your family.

DEUTERONOMY 26:11 MSG

Does not all nature around me praise God? If I were silent, I should be an exception to the universe. Does not the thunder praise Him as it rolls like drums in the march of the God of armies?... Does not the lightning write His name in letters of fire? Has not the whole earth a voice? And shall I, can I, silent be?

CHARLES H. SPURGEON

The heavens declare the glory of God;
And the firmament shows His handiwork.

PSALM 19:1 NKJV

What matters supremely is not the fact that I know God, but the larger fact which underlies it—the fact that He knows me.... I am never out of His mind.... I know Him because He first knew me, and continues to know me.

J. I. PACKER

You have searched me, LORD, and you know me. You know when I sit and when I rise; you perceive my thoughts from afar. You discern my going out and my lying down; you are familiar with all my ways.

PSALM 139:1–3 NIV

Live for today but hold your hands open to tomorrow. Anticipate the future and its changes with joy. There is a seed of God's love in every event, every circumstance...in which you may find yourself.

BARBARA JOHNSON

God is the one who provides seed for the farmer and then bread to eat. In the same way, he will provide and increase your resources and then produce a great harvest of generosity in you.

2 CORINTHIANS 9:10 NLT

In difficulties, I can drink freely of God's power and experience His touch of refreshment and blessing—much like an invigorating early spring rain.

ANABEL GILLHAM

As for me, I shall sing of Your strength; yes, I shall joyfully sing of Your lovingkindness in the morning, for You have been my stronghold.

PSALM 59:16 NASB

The miracle of joy is this: It happens when there is no apparent reason for it. Circumstances may call for despair. Yet something different rouses itself inside us.... We remember God. We remember He is love. We remember He is near.

RUTH SENTER

Satisfy us in the morning with your unfailing love,
that we may sing for joy and be glad all our days.

PSALM 90:14 NIV

We need more than a watchmaker who winds up the universe and lets it tick. We need love and mercy and forgiveness and grace—qualities only a personal God can offer.

PHILIP YANCEY

God makes everything come out right; he puts victims back on their feet....
He doesn't endlessly nag and scold, nor hold grudges forever. He doesn't treat
us as our sins deserve, nor pay us back in full for our wrongs. As high as heaven is
over the earth, so strong is his love to those who fear him.

Psalm 103:6, 9–11 msg

Look deep within yourself and recognize what brings life and grace into your heart. It is this that can be shared with those around you. You are loved by God. This is an inspiration to love.

CHRISTOPHER DE VINCK

May you have the power to understand, as all God's people should,
how wide, how long, how high, and how deep his love is.

Being able to bow in prayer as the day begins or ends gives expression to the frustrations and concerns that might not otherwise be ventilated. On the other end of that prayer line is a loving heavenly Father who has promised to hear and answer our petitions.

JAMES DOBSON

Cast your burden on the LORD,
And he shall sustain you.

PSALM 55:22 NKJV

Each one of us is God's special work of art. Through us, He teaches and inspires, delights and encourages, informs and uplifts all those who view our lives.

Joni Eareckson Tada

For we are God's masterpiece. He has created us anew in Christ Jesus, so we can do the good things he planned for us long ago.

EPHESIANS 2:10 NLT

Our hearts were made for joy. Our hearts were made to enjoy the One who created them. Too deeply planted to be much affected by the ups and downs of life, this joy is a knowing and a being known by our Creator. He sets our hearts alight with radiant joy.

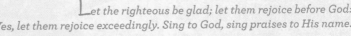

*Let the righteous be glad; let them rejoice before God:
Yes, let them rejoice exceedingly. Sing to God, sing praises to His name.*

Psalm 68:3-4 NKJV

God cannot give us a happiness and peace apart from Himself, because it is not there. There is no such thing.

C. S. Lewis

God's peace...is far more wonderful than the human mind can understand. His peace will keep your thoughts and your hearts quiet and at rest.

PHILIPPIANS 4:7 TLB

Heaven often seems distant and unknown,
but if He who made the road...is our guide,
we need not fear to lose the way.

HENRY VAN DYKE

I will lead the blind by ways they have not known, along unfamiliar paths I will guide them; I will turn the darkness into light before them and make the rough places smooth. These are the things I will do; I will not forsake them.

ISAIAH 42:16 NIV

To be grateful is to recognize the Love of God in everything He has given us— and He has given us everything. Every breath we draw is a gift of His love, every moment of existence is a gift of grace.

THOMAS MERTON

Isn't everything you have and everything you are sheer gifts from God?

1 CORINTHIANS 4:7 MSG

God guides us, despite our uncertainties and our vagueness, even through our failings and mistakes.... He leads us step by step, from event to event. Only afterwards...when we survey the whole progress of our lives, do we experience the feeling of having been led without knowing it, the feeling that God has mysteriously guided us.

PAUL TOURNIER

Those who know your name trust in you, for you, LORD, have never forsaken those who seek you.

PSALM 9:10 NIV

Ellie Claire® Gift & Paper Expressions
Brentwood, TN 37027
EllieClaire.com

Better Is One Day Journal
© 2014 by Ellie Claire
Ellie Claire is a registered trademark of Worthy Media, Inc.

ISBN 978-1-60936-931-6

Stock or custom editions of Ellie Claire titles may be purchased in bulk for educational, business, ministry, fundraising, or sales promotional use. For information, please e-mail info@EllieClaire. com.

Compiled by Connie Troyer.
Cover and interior design by Gearbox | StudioGearbox.com

Printed in China.

1 2 3 4 5 6 7 8 9 – 19 18 17 16 15 14